SKYLINERS

Dedication

To

E.B. Hummel—aviator *par excellence*, who flew a number of the airliners pictured herein

David P. Morgan—writer *extraordinaire*, who had the opportunity to ride on many of these airplanes, and to share his experiences with us in his unique style

Text copyright George W. Hamlin, 1991

All rights reserved. No part of this book may be reproduced in any form or by any means without the prior written permission of the publisher.

Designed by Sharon Gardner, Gardner Graphics

Edited & Produced by John Wegg

Typesetting by Al Beechick, Arrow Connection

Color Separations & Printing by Scott Piazza, The Drawing Board

Manufactured in Hong Kong

Published by
World Transport Press, Inc
PO Box 521238
Miami, Florida 33152-1238
USA

ISBN 0-9626730-1-3

Introduction

Do you remember the airline industry of the late 1950s/early 1960s, when four-engined pistons coexisted with their jet replacements? When large turboprops had a future, because jets weren't applicable on short-haul routes? Or when carrier marketing focused on equipment types, and colorful, complex paint schemes?

If you do share an interest in this fascinating era in the airline business, it's likely that you never expected to see it again, in all its glory. About all that's left are publicity photos, generally showing a brand new piece of equipment flying serenely over a scenic landscape, or, together with professional models posing as passengers.

What's missing is the view you might have gotten from the observation deck at your local airport—a Connie here, DC-7 there, with a brand new Electra behind, together with several DC-3s from Local-Service carriers. While the PR shots do preserve the basics, they don't have as much ability to call up the evocative memories of air travel during what might be termed its adolescent years.

Fortunately, someone did preserve this maturing industry in its natural habitat; we can thank Mel Lawrence for being there with his camera, and recording both the commonplace and the unusual for us to enjoy. Mel was one of a very small number of photographers to focus, in a serious way, on the airlines of the time. While isolated snapshots of the era exist, the slides he shot offer one of the few chances to revisit the commercial airports of the '50s and '60s on an extensive basis, in living color.

So, without further ado, let's get on to what you've come for—a time machine tour of the airlines and airports of North America from east coast to west. Enjoy!

George W. Hamlin

Acknowledgments

A number of people provided advice about and encouragement for this project, including my wife, Kali; John Wegg, who in addition to editing, also provided the detailed aircraft histories; Bryant Petitt, Bruce Drum and Keith Armes; Dick Wallin, who located the photos; and last, but not least, Mel Lawrence, for being there with his camera. The photos included are from the collections of Mel Lawrence and George Hamlin.

Welcome aboard! We hope that you enjoy this photographic journey around North America during the airline industry's piston to jet transition. Fasten your seat belts, sit back and relax, and enjoy the trip. (Continental's marketing department is not going to let the first-class passengers board this Boeing 707-124 at Denver without being fully aware of which carrier they are using; and of course, stainless steel handrails just won't do for a 'Golden Jet'.)

N74612 was the 57th 707 off Boeing's Renton line. Delivered to Continental in March 1960, it later saw service with TWA. Subsequently sold to Israel and used by the Israel Defence Forces, it was acquired by the Israel Airports Authority in 1983 and used as a ground trainer at Tel Aviv.

Long ago, but not so far away, the jet age began for US carriers at a familiar location whose name many no longer recognize—Idlewild, as New York's JFK International was known until Christmas Eve 1963. Pan Am, of course, was the operator; the Boeing 707-121, the aircraft. One of the originals (note it lacks the ventral fin modification), N709PA thrusts itself into the sky in July 1959, quite obviously prior to its conversion to 'fanjet' power.

Jet Clipper America (later Jet Clipper Tradewind) was the third production Boeing 707 to be built. Delivered to Pan American in 1958, it was lost in a crash at Elkton, Maryland, on December 8, 1963. The probable cause was a lightning strike which ignited fuel tank vapor.

Most other denizens of IDL at the time relied on propellers, such as this Trans Caribbean DC-4 and DC-6A freighter duo. The latter shows evidence of its owner, Canadian Pacific, in the form of its livery and *Empress of Santa Maria* name; TCA did not offer scheduled service to the Azores. In fact, the former Supplemental Air Carrier was not widely known outside the northeast US, and, of course, the Caribbean, although it competed with both Eastern and Pan Am with enough success to remain in business until its 1971 absorption into American Airlines.

N75416 Manuel Tous (actually an ex USAAF C-54A Skymaster) was leased by TCA to Eastern and Transocean for brief periods. After a short spell in Germany with Continentale in the early 1960s, it ended up with broker California Airmotive which scrapped it. Built for Canadian Pacific in 1958, DC-6A N45500 was leased by TCA between 1959 and 1961, then by World Airways and Saturn. Following a period of ownership by NWT Air, it passed to Ethiopian Airlines. After 34,552 flying hours it was retired and is now with the airline's mechanics training school at Addis Ababa.

Both of Trans Carib's competitors fielded piston equipment of their own at IDL in this time period, examples being provided by one of Eastern's large fleet of 'Silver Falcon' Martin 404s . . .

In company with several of its brethren, Martin 404 N469A was acquired by Southern Airways. It was scrapped at Atlanta in 1971.

. . . and Pan Am's DC-7C *Clipper Blackhawk*—in the carrier's parlance, a 'Super 7', although the model was referred to elsewhere as the 'Seven Seas'. This type would prove to be extremely vulnerable to the jets, although it held a decided nonstop range advantage over the earliest 707s and DC-8s.

Manufactured on August 25, 1956, DC-7C N732PA went on to a charter career with Intercontinental Air, Air Trans Africa (of Rhodesia), and Trans Europa of Spain. It was completely broken up at Madrid on November 14, 1974.

Although never a major factor, turboprops or propjets put in appearances at New York International as well; an example is provided by Northwest's Electra, N123US.

Lockheed 188C Electra N123US was later used by Air California. Sold to Mandala Airlines in 1979, it is still in service with the Indonesian carrier.

A more unusual mode of transport was represented by New York Airways' Vertol 44B, shown here at the American terminal in close proximity to a jet 'Flagship'.

One of five Vertol 44Bs used by NYA between 1958 and 1962, N10100 was traded-in to Boeing Vertol for Model 107s along with the other NYA 44Bs.

It's now April 1964, and the name and code have changed, to JFK, but other features, such as the Northeast DC-3 shown here, continue traditions started much earlier. As one of the smaller Trunks, and one with a number of short-haul routes to re-gional destinations, the carrier would operate the classic twin (this one has been upgraded with a main landing gear door conversion kit) later than most other carriers in its category.

DC3A (C-53D-DO) N44992 was built in 1943 at Santa Monica as a C-53D-DO and used by United immediately after the war. Disposed of by Northeast in 1967, it is still registered to North Cay Airways in Puerto Rico.

More and more of the long-haul operations at JFK by this time were jets, of course, as represented by this trio of DC-8s. A DC-8-32 from Pan Am's launch order for the type . . .

Jet Clipper Great Republic was operated by Pan American from June 1960 until October 1968, when it was sold to United Airlines as N8246U. Subsequently, it passed to Overseas National Airways, then was converted to an all-freighter and used by Rosenbalm Aviation and Emery Worldwide. It was broken up at Miami in January 1986 after flying over 48,000 hours and completing nearly 24,000 flights.

. . . National's Series 32 N7183C (with its previous identity, N804US, still visible on the fuselage) —although National had the honor of the first domestic scheduled jet service, with a leased Pan Am 707, its own fleet relied on the Douglas product . . .

Purchased from Northwest by National, N7183C later served with Overseas National Airways and was broken up in 1977.

... and, a long way from its predecessors pictured earlier, Trans Carib's fan-powered Jet Trader (DC-8F-54) N8783R *Peter Jonathan II.*

Delivered to Trans Carib in December 1963, N8783R was acquired by American Airlines with its takeover of TCA in May 1971. However, AA never used DC-8s and after a period of storage at Fort Worth, '83R was leased to Seaboard World Airlines. In 1975, it became one of the few DC-8s ever registered in the UK (with IAS Cargo Airlines). With its Pratt & Whitney JT3Bs now hushkitted, it is still in service today, operated by Miami-based Agro Air on behalf of Interamericana.

Across the Hudson River in New Jersey, a parallel transition could be observed at Newark, although the emphasis here was clearly on domestic and regional operations. As a result, a visit to the observation deck was likely to yield views of Allegheny DC-3s and Martin 202s (overleaf).

N147A, a Long Beach-built C-47A, was acquired by Allegheny's predecessor, All-American Airways, in 1948. After 12 years in Local-Service operation it was sold to the Haiti Air Force and may still be active.

Ex Northwest Martin 202 N171A was traded-in to Fairchild-Hiller in 1966 for F-27Js. It was scrapped at Wildwood, New Jersey, 11 years later.

Future Allegheny merger partner Mohawk provided its 'Air Chief' Convairs, such as the 240 shown here. Circa 1960, who would have con-templated the AL/MO amalgamation or, for that matter, the survivor's operation of transcon non-stops, or flights to Europe?

Air Chief Pequot, a Convair 240-11 originally delivered to Swissair, was another trade-in for F-27Js. It was scrapped during the 1980s.

Even the Trunks reflected the more localized atmosphere at EWR, with United operating a number of its distinctive Caravelle VIR (6R) fleet here. Newark was, in fact, the New York origin/destination of the carrier's premier 'Executive' service with this equipment—an all-first-class, extra fare ($3.00!), 'for men only' operation to and from Chicago's O'Hare (female flight attendants were apparently tolerated, however!).

Caravelle N1016U Ville de Nantes *returned to Europe in 1972 upon sale by United to Sterling Airways of Denmark. After only a few months of Scandinavian charter service, it went home to France and was used by Catair and Europe Aero Service until it was broken up at Paris-Orly in 1980.*

At the other end of what would become known as the Northeast Corridor, Washington National retained a strong prop flavor at the beginning of the jet age, since its short runways could not accommodate the early jets. From July 1959, Allegheny made brief use of the Napier Eland 'Jet-Prop' conversion of the Convair twins, called the Convair 540, and so became the first Local-Service airline to operate a turbine-powered type. One of these forerunners of the more successful 580/600 series conversions sits at DCA in the summer of 1962, minus titles, but clearly in AL's colors.

N544Z was built for United as a Convair 340-31. Converted to 540 standard in 1960 for Allegheny, it reverted to piston power as an upgraded 440. Sold in 1963, it became an Allison-powered 580 for AVENSA and until recently was operated by Intair in Canada.

Eastern aircraft were very frequent visitors to Washington. In addition to Martin 404s *(page 7)*, EA also operated the similarly-sized Convair 440.

Convair 440-86 N9320 was passed on to Mackey in Florida then several private owners. In 1989, it was still registered to a Miami-based concern.

Four-engined products of both Douglas and Lockheed manufacture were featured in the Eastern fleet, also. Representing the Lockheed family,

'Super G' N6239G displays the less-common red fuselage colors utilized by dedicated Air-Shuttle Connies.

After ten years with Eastern, N6239G's active life was over and it was scrapped at Miami in 1967.

By 1963, Piedmont had moved up to Martins as their prime aircraft. Two pose here on the DCA ramp; check out the United Viscounts to the rear, as well!

Ex Eastern Martin 404 N40444 West Virginia Centennial 1863-1963 Pacemaker *(later* New River Pacemaker*) was retired in 1969 and subsequently scrapped at Charlotte, North Carolina.*

Miami International has long been Mecca for the airline enthusiast; the next seven views from the 1959-62 period help explain why. Leading off are shots of one of the least known US international carriers—PANAGRA. Half-owned each by Pan Am and the W.R. Grace Company—hence the acronym—Pan American Grace Airways provided service to the west coast of South America. The featured 'El Inter Americano' service was provided with DC-7Bs like N51700 . . .

The first of six DC-7Bs delivered to PANAGRA, N51700 was used for an extensive press tour around South America when the airline introduced the type into service in 1955. After 11 years with PANAGRA and brief use by the Carolina Vagabonds, it was sold to the Atlanta Skylarks, another travel club, and broken up for spares.

. . . while PANAGRA's 'El Pacifico' tourist trips
were the domain of DC-6Bs such as N6537C.

*DC-6B N6537C later served with Standard Airways and Pacific Western and eventually became a fire bomber with Conair of British
Columbia. It was scrapped in 1984.*

National, whose home base was at MIA, was a major factor there. Representing the 'Airline of the Stars' are a DC-7 and a Super H Constellation, and *(overleaf)* an Electra.

N8205H is a straight DC-7 built in 1953. Like tens of other Sevens, it was scrapped by California Airmotive at Fox Field, Lancaster, California.

Built as a Model 188A, N5002K was converted as a pure-freighter after it had left National's service. Operated by Great Northern Airlines (originally Fairbanks Air) from 1974, it crashed at Lake Udrivik, Alaska, on March 12, 1976.

The 'Airline of the Stars' slogan was held over to the initial jet livery, shown on DC-8-51 N774C, complete with a two-tone star; the red carpet awaiting the DC-8's passengers was a feature which didn't survive as long as this aircraft in NA's service, however.

Operated by National Airlines for ten years, N774C was sold to Braniff and broken up at Miami in January 1983.

In July 1959, Capital had not been absorbed into United, and was capable of putting on the display visible here—two Connies, with a pair of its trademark Viscounts in the background. The Delta DC-6 and DC-7 don't detract from the view, either!

Prior to acquisition by Capital Airlines in 1955 as N2739A Fleet No. 759, this Model 49 had operated with American Overseas Airlines, Pan American, and BOAC. After a total of 31,686 hours, it was retired in September 1960 and subsequently broken up at Trenton, New Jersey.

In contrast with its name, Northeast maintained a significant presence, and crew base, in Miami. This reflected the fact that a large proportion of the airline's passenger miles were in the Florida market, as opposed to short-hauls in its native New England. The equipment dominant on the long-hauls prior to the arrival of 'Yellowbird' 727s was the Convair 880; a pair sun themselves at MIA in May 1962.

Leased by Northeast for nearly three years from TWA, N8481H is currently one of the ex TWA 880s parked at Mojave, California.

New Orleans in 1959 may not have had quite the variety of Miami, but the sights of two elderly piston twins—a Southern DC-3, and a Delta C-46 freighter, are worth a brief side trip, at least. The DC-3 has just arrived on Flight 355 from Memphis, Greenville, Monroe, Natchez, and Baton Rouge. Not content with the normal designation, note that DL has re-christened the Curtiss product as a 'Super D-46' Air Freighter.

N85SA was built as a C-53D-DO in 1943 and acquired by Southern in 1954 from Continental Airlines. It is currently registered in the US to a private owner in Ohio.

Built as a C-46D at Buffalo, New York, in 1945, Delta's N9873F Fleet No.101 had seen service with Civil Air Transport in the Far East and had been upgraded to a more powerful 'C-46R' by Riddle. It was last heard of in Zaire with Congofrigo.

Further up the Mississippi, Southern propliners were well represented at Memphis, also, circa 1965. DC-3 N66SA has just arrived from Columbus and Tupelo as Flight 101 (note designator in the window just forward of the passenger door), while sister N87A *(opposite)* is parked behind one of its owner's Martin 404 'Aristocrats'.

With Southern from 1954 until 1967, ex Continental C-53D N66SA was still on the US register (as N31MS) in 1990, registered to an owner in the Miami area.

DC3A (C-53D-DO) N87SA had already seen service with Pennsylvania Central Airlines, Capital, and Continental before Southern acquired it in 1954. It is currently registered to a Fort Lauderdale-based concern.

Ex Eastern 404 N259S has been a Florida resident since 1976, when it was acquired by Shawnee Airlines. After operating with Florida Airlines, associate Ocean Airways, and successor Southern International Airways, it was sold to Systems-International Airways.

While both Piedmont and Southern supplanted the DC-3 with the 404, their choice of jet equipment was very different. Southern opted for the Douglas DC-9, while PI waited for the later 737 and eventually became a major operator of the type). An August 1969 visit to MEM provides visual evidence, in the form of SO's N93S, and Piedmont's 'short pipe' 737, N735N.

DC-9-15 N93S, through two company acquisitions, now serves Northwest.

Boeing 737-201 N735N Appalachian Pacemaker *likewise survived a company takeover and now flies for USAir as N202AU.*

Also to be seen at Memphis was another Regional's new jet equipment, in the form of Texas International's DC-9-30 'Pamper Jet', N1309T.

DC-9-31 N1309T (at one time City of Austin) *served with TI's associates, New York Air and Continental, and is now with Northwest.*

Chicago's Midway Airport was, in the summer of 1959, both at its peak, and about to reach its nadir. As the principal airport at the country's primary connecting point for east-west travel, it held the title of 'world's busiest' during the piston era. Soon, however, O'Hare, because of its jet-suitable runways, would eclipse its older neighbor. In the interim enjoy the show at MDW, beginning with a four-page collection of Local-Service carrier DC-3s.

Modified with streamlined gear doors, N139D was a genuine pre-war ex TWA DC3B-202A. It was written-off at Malcolm Island, Saskatoon, on July 10, 1969, four years after Ozark had disposed of it.

Coincidentally, North Central's N18949 Fleet No. 16, was also built for TWA (as a DC3-209A) just one month before Ozark's N139D, in December 1937. Moving to the private sector in 1967, it crashed at West Deering, New Hampshire, on June 24, 1981.

Yet another DC3 (a -269 for Northwest), Lake Central's N21711 was sold to Zamrud of Bali, Indonesia, in 1968. The Gooney Bird was not long in paradise, it crashed at Sumbawa Besar on August 20, 1972. North Central's N12954, Fleet No. 27 (center background), was laid down as a DC3-454 for the Netherlands East Indies Air Force but impressed by the USAAF as a C-49J. Immediately after the war, it was Eastern's Fleet No. 386; it is still on the US register. Ozark N134D (right background) was a C-53D-DO and postwar served with American and Western; it too is still registered.

DC3A-453 N45335 was built for United but went straight to military service as a C-53C. Mid-Continent and Braniff used it before Lake Central and it was destroyed in a hangar fire at Indianapolis, Indiana, on November 1, 1963.

By this time, the Trunks' smallest equipment was generally in the Convair-Liner category, as represented by American's 240 *Flagship Lone Star State . . .*

Later converted to Rolls-Royce Dart power as a Convair 600 for Trans-Texas Airways, N94253 went on to operate with SMB Stage Lines, Royal American Airways, and Bar Harbor. It has been withdrawn from use for many years.

. . . and Delta's 440 N4814C (originally delivered to DL as a 340). Check out the sporty 440 Falcon parked on the other side of the runway as well!

Originally built as a 340, N4814C left the Delta fleet in 1970 and after spells with Aspen Airways and Sierra Pacific Airlines, is now hauling copies of the Wall Street Journal *for Dow Jones.*

Larger pistons were in evidence, also; witness Braniff's DC-6 . . .

A 1947-vintage DC-6, N90884 went south to Aviateca of Guatemala in 1966. Thirteen years later, it was seized by the Broward County, Florida, Sheriff's Department after being discovered abandoned in a field and containing marijuana residue! After a ferry flight to Fort Lauderdale and storage, it was scrapped in 1981.

... and an Eastern DC-7B, complete with a 'Falcon Super Coach' sticker. Interestingly, the term 'Super Coach' would resurface in the Chicago market again in the late 1970s, when TWA applied the term to a short-lived pricing experiment using high density seating 707s in the Los Angeles market.

With Eastern from 1958 to 1965, N844D met its fate—like so many Sevens—in the hands of California Airmotive at Fox Field, Lancaster, California.

PAGE 44

While not suitable for jets, Midway was a marvelous place to watch the brief fling the Trunks had with the turboprop. Eastern's 'Golden Falcon' Electra surely is the epitome of 1950s airline style.

Electra N5525 is still in service today, with Zantop International Airlines as a freighter (registered N344HA).

The British propjets were also featured at MDW, and the TCA Vickers Viscount is 'foreign' in more than manufacture.

Viscount 757 CF-THL, Fleet No. 630, operated with TCA and Air Canada for nearly 17 years; it was subsequently scrapped.

The Viscount will always be most heavily associated in the US with one carrier—Capital. Fleet Number 365, N7446, poses for its portrait in front of a TWA Connie and a pair of American Convair 240s, while *(overleaf)* sister ship No. 330 undergoes maintenance next to a company DC-3.

Built in 1956, V.745D N7446 went on to United service after the acquisition of Capital in 1961 and was eventually scrapped at Burbank, California, in 1968 after nearly 26,000 flying hours.

Another 1956-built Viscount 745D, Fleet No. 330 (N7411) also saw service with United. Along with several other United Viscounts, it was scrapped at Georgetown, Delaware. The DC3-313C in the background, N25689 Fleet No. 211B, is still around and currently registered to General Services of Boca Raton, Florida.

The victor in the Chicago airport contest, O'Hare, naturally featured jet equipment. While the livery carried on Eastern's DC-8-21 N8617 is not quite as fancy as that originally applied to the Electras, it's certainly a far cry from the later 'Hockey Stick' scheme.

N8617 was acquired by Overseas National Airways (as N819F) in 1973 after 12 years service with Eastern. Five years later it was converted to an all-freighter, but by the mid-1980s it had come to the end of its useful life and it was broken up at that well-known airliner graveyard—Miami.

Two of the United types found at ORD on a frequent basis—the Caravelle and 720—face off here.

Ville de Saintes, *United's sixth Caravelle VIR (6R), was later used by Sterling Airways of Denmark, and Transavia Holland, both charter companies. In 1974, it was acquired by the African Republic of Mauritania as a VIP aircraft and after several years of few flying hours it is now parked at Dakar, Senegal, awaiting its inevitable fate of becoming aluminum scrap metal. Boeing 720-022 N7220U fared better as it is now in the hands of the apprentices of the George T. Baker Aviation School, Miami, after a second career in Europe (with Belgium's Delta Air Transport) and a third career in Central America.*

One concourse over, a Braniff 720 departs in front of a Northwest DC-7, and provides graphic evidence of US airlines' infatuation with red, white and blue color schemes.

Boeing 720-048 N7081 was acquired by Braniff in 1964 from Aer Lingus. Two years later, it passed to Pacific Northern Airlines and spent most of the remainder of its life in that part of the US, with PNA, Western, Alaska Airlines, and Aeroamerica. It was broken up at Boeing Field, just a few miles from its birthplace, in 1980.

O'Hare wasn't exclusively jet in 1965, and other colors were in use as well. Ozark fielded both piston and turboprop equipment at its Chicago terminus, in the form of a Martin 404 and a trio of F-27s.

Once with Eastern and then Mohawk, N463M went to Fairchild Hiller in part-trade for F-27s and storage at Las Vegas, Nevada, in 1967. It never left the shade of the casinos and was recycled for aluminum ten years later.

Delivered to Ozark in 1959, F-27 N4302F was returned to Fairchild Hiller ten years later. Later with Southeast Airlines in Florida, it has now been retired. The ex Capital Viscount 745D (N7407) in United service was another of the aircraft scrapped at Georgetown, Delaware.

Our next stop is Dallas' Love Field, but please permit a slight diversion to neighboring Fort Worth, to look at Continental's Convair 240 N94238. Sure, you were able to discern that the aircraft used to fly for American just by the red trim on the nacelles, right?

Originally with American Airlines, Convair 240-0 N94238 was leased by Continental from Dundel Corp for six months in 1959. Subsequently, it was used by Toa Domestic of Japan, Cordova Airlines, and Alaska Airlines. It was scrapped at Long Beach, California, in the early 1980s.

Love Field in the early 1960s had it all, from the point of view of the airline watcher, from the traditional props to the newest jets, all eminently viewable from the terminal's excellent observation deck. For starters, how about Trans-Texas DC-3s in both bare metal and *(overleaf)* white crown schemes—the former still with its original right-hand door configuration and the latter a 'Super-Starliner'.

An American Airlines DC3-277D acquired by TTA in 1947, N33654 was modified to DC3A standard by replacing its original Wright GR-1820 Cyclone engines with Pratt & Whitney R-1830 Twin Wasps. Air New England operated it from 1971 to 1977, then Cryder-man Air Services/Century Airlines, of Pontiac, Michigan, took it over. The aircraft was stripped for spares in 1986.

Built with a left-hand door for Braniff, DC3-314A N25668 also became a DC3A. A true Texan (TTA took '668 over from Braniff in 1953 and operated it for 15 years), the Three was eventually broken up at San Antonio.

TTA's 'big' equipment at the time was the Convair 240; N94216 departs in February 1962, with but a sole jet visible.

The 28th Convair-Liner off the San Diego line, 240-0 N94216 was built for American. It was later converted to a Dart-powered 600 (see page 78) and saw service with Bar Harbor. It is no longer active, although still registered.

Central was another Local-Service carrier operating the Douglas and Convair twins at Love, in close juxtaposition to Braniff aircraft of all three modes of propulsion. One of the baggage handlers seems to be working somewhat harder than his compatriots!

Built as a right-hand door DC3-207 for United in 1937, N287SE is thought to have been scrapped in 1988.

Convair 240-0 N74854 was acquired from American Airlines by Central in 1962 and four years later was converted to a Dart Convair 600. It was active as a freighter with SMB Stage Line until 1989.

The Trunk carriers were undergoing their own piston to jet transition. Over at Delta's gates, for example, you could still see yeoman DC-6s, together with later DC-7s. The Sevens carried 'DC-7 Golden Crown' titles on the nose, in case you managed, through diligent effort, to miss the rather large depictions on the tail.

The 80th DC-6, N37531 was acquired by Delta from United in 1958 as Fleet No. 623. Disposed of ten years later, it was eventually scrapped at Tucson, Arizona.

Like most other Delta DC-7s, N4873C Fleet No. 703, was sold to BMR Aviation which chopped them at Ontario, California, in the late 1960s.

Delta's early jets came in two different color schemes. The DC-8-10s featured white on top, and natural metal below. The Convair 880s, on the other hand, were decked out in white both above and below the blue cheat line. Nacelle decorations were still in vogue in January 1963; note how each type reflects the tail insignia.

DC-8-12 (ex -11 and later a -51) N803E was operating recently in the Dominican Republic with Aerochago.

Convair 880 N8814E operated with Delta for ten years until traded-in to Boeing (for 727s). It has spent the same amount of time parked at Mojave, California.

Like its future Dallas hub competitor, American also utilized DC-6s at Love during this time period, but AA had quite a different philosophy with regard to painting aircraft. Achieving good results with natural metal finishes requires frequent polishing—something N90748 *Flagship Wilkes-Barre* certainly doesn't lack.

Disposed of by American in 1965, N90748 flew with Austral in Argentina before it was traded-in in part-payment for NAMC YS-11s. The Japanese manufacturer contracted Aero Tech to break up '748 at its old home—Fort Worth—in December 1970.

American also brought its Electras as far west as Texas; N6126A *Flagship Tucson* stands ready to go in front of DC-6 N90748 on another occasion.

Flown by American for a decade from 1960, Model 188A Electra N6126A was subsequently converted as a freighter and is still active today with TPI International Airways.

While Delta favored traditional supplier Douglas for its initial fleet of 'large' jets, American turned to Boeing and its 707. American quickly converted its aircraft to fan power when it became available, including -123B N7526A.

After 17 years with American, N7526A moved to England with Monarch Airlines, then south to Cyprus Airways, and then west with AERONICA of Nicaragua.

America's 'Leading Airline' (by its own admission) did share Delta's interest in Convair jets, although it chose the later—and racier—Convair 990. The transition to the jet age apparently had no impact on AA's skin-polishing habits!

America's 'Leading Airline' (by its own admission) did share Delta's interest in Convair jets, although it chose the later—and racier—Convair 990. The transition to the jet age apparently had no impact on AA's skin-polishing habits!

Convair 990A (Model 30A) N5611 saw only five years service with American before being sold to Spanish charter operator Spantax. After Spantax ceased operations, its Coronado fleet was grounded at Palma de Mallorca. Scrapping of eleven of the dozen 990s started in early 1991.

Hometown carrier Braniff in many ways mirrored its larger rival American in equipment choices, with four-engined Douglas pistons and Electras in the prop category. Since Love was BN's home base,

the display could be stunning—witness N91311 passing four fellow propliners, while Electra N9708C heads out past that other airline's hangar.

Ex Western DC-6B N91311 was sold to LAN Chile in 1965, then passed on to TAME (Transportes Aéreos Militares Ecuatorianas) in 1971.

Model 188A Electra N9708C was sold in 1969 via Boeing to LANSA of Peru. On August 9 the following year, it struck a mountain after take-off from Cuzco.

Braniff's original jets simply carried on with the piston-era livery, such as on N7075, a 707-227 waiting to depart on Flight 31 to Houston.

One of only five -227s built, N7095 stayed with Braniff until 1971 when it was sold to BWIA (British West Indian Airways). Four years later it was placed in storage and subsequently broken up.

The carrier's introduction of the 'end of the plain plane' marketing campaign certainly could not be said to mirror anyone else, however. The fleet, including these 720s *(also overleaf)*, was out-fitted in a variety of pastel hues, with ground equipment to match.

N7079 was sold by Braniff to American Aviation Services in 1973 which leased it out to two travel clubs, Club International and Ambassadair International, then to Seattle-based Aeroamerica. It was finally broken up at Bournemouth, England, in 1982.

Aeroamerica also leased N7077 from American Aviation Services until it was retired in 1981 and scrapped at Boeing Field, Seattle. Coincidentally, the blue 720 in the background, N7083, also flew with Aeroamerica and met the same fate at the same airport. However, it was originally an Aer Lingus aircraft and only leased by Braniff for a year.

White nacelles were included, as well, as shown on one of BN's unique 707-227s (the 707-200 was a -100 with more powerful JT4A engines). The turquoise color was unique in airline circles also; the sobriquets 'Easter egg/jelly bean airline' were not entirely without merit during this period!

Like sister ship N7095, N7074 was also acquired by BWIA. It then went through several owners, including Club Alaska, before meeting the melting pot at Moses Lake, Washington, in 1981.

By the late 1960s, operations at Love showed evidence of transition in the airline world. Braniff, of course, was still both well represented and colorful. The Electras survived long enough to be painted in the pastels, while the machine which would eventually dominate the carrier's domestic operations—the 727—had made its debut, as well.

N9704C also went to LANSA (see page 69) and suffered a similar sudden fate. On December 24, 1971, it crashed on approach to Puerto Inca.

Boeing 727-116 was built for LAN Chile but not delivered and leased by Boeing to Braniff for just seven months in 1969. Subsequently, it was purchased by Mexicana then operated by Aerotal Colombia. It was still active with Alaska Airlines (as N7829A) in 1991.

That Frontier 727 in front of the Braniff party? Well, FL had absorbed Central, and like the other Local-Service carriers—now termed Regionals— had entered the jet age, and begun to compete directly with the Trunks.

Boeing 727-191 N7271F had a three-year career with Frontier then returned to the manufacturers. After a lease period with Braniff, it served with Regent Air, the short-lived luxury carrier, and now flies with its successor, MGM Grand Air.

The Trunks, meanwhile, were in the process of disposing of their remaining pistons and turboprops. At American, the smaller short-range equipment was supplanted by the BAC One-Eleven 400, which American termed its '400 Astrojet'. It's doubtful that the towbar on the left will be useful with this pocket rocket, however.

Delivered to American in December 1965, N5015 went into storage six years later. Since 1973, it has operated as a corporate aircraft and is currently owned by NPC Leasing (as N56B).

Transition also had come to Trans-Texas, both in the form of in-kind upgrade of the Convairs, from 240s to Rolls-Royce-powered 'Silver Cloud' 600s, and in the addition of 'Pamper Jet' DC-9s. Further ahead: a name change to Texas International, and a more colorful, Texas-patriotic, paint scheme.

N94216 (see also page 57) was sold to Bar Harbor Airlines in 1979; it is now inactive.

Originally built as a DC-9-15 Multiple Change passenger/cargo version (DC-9-15F(MC)), N1303T passed on to Finnair and was converted to a pure-freighter in 1981. It is now operated by Evergreen International in the same role.

After departing Dallas, how about a quick diversion via the Rocky Mountain states prior to landing on the West Coast? At Denver, a pair of Convair 340s awaits—Frontier's *Sunliner Zuni* and United's *Mainliner Sacramento*.

Built for United as a 340-31, N73129 was converted with Allison turboprops to 580 standard (a designation that originated with Frontier) in 1964. It is still working for a living with ERA Aviation of Anchorage, Alaska.

Mainliner Sacramento *(Convair 340-31 N73109) also wound up as a 580 and until 1990 was in service with Aspen Airways—coincidentally operating as a United Express.*

By 1969, even Great Falls, Montana, had entered the jet age, as evidenced by the simultaneous presence of two Western 737s, in the airline's classic 'Indian Head' livery. Two-zero-seven is early in its career, as indicated by the original stubby nacelles.

Boeing 737-247 N4507W served with Western until its merger with Delta in 1987. A year later it was acquired by the 'new' Braniff but since that company's second failure, it has been put out to tumbleweed at Mojave, California.

While today's Los Angeles International conjures up images of Jumbo Jets and Pacific Rim carriers, LAX in the late 1950s was a place where piston airliners could be viewed in all their glory. One of the more fondly remembered types was the Boeing 377 Stratocruiser, seen here in the familiar Pan Am, no, Pan American World Airways, scheme. This is *"Strato" Clipper Flying Cloud*, as indicated both on the nose and aft of the main entry door.

The 19th Stratocruiser built, N1028V was delivered to Pan American in 1949. In 1961, it was traded-in to Boeing for 707s and became a freighter with RANSA (Rutas Aéreas Nacionales SA) of Venezuela. Following the bankruptcy of RANSA in 1966, it was scrapped at Miami.

Here's another classic—TWA's 749 Connie, the *Star of Israel*, passing a couple of its Douglas competitors in the background.

N91209 spent its whole 18-year career with TWA and in December 1966, after 40,665 hours, it was withdrawn from use at Fairfax Airport, Kansas City. Two years later it was scrapped on the same site.

Flanked by other TWA Constellations is a Continental 'Club Coach' DC-7B, used by its owner on prime nonstop routes to Denver, Kansas City and Chicago from LAX.

The second N8210H (the first was destroyed in a mid-air collision with a USAF Northrop F-89 Scorpion over southern California prior to delivery), DC-7B City of Chicago *was retired to the Tallmantz Aviation Museum at Orange County. Unfortunately, it was later scrapped.*

Slightly older Douglases were in evidence also, including DC-6Bs from Western and United, with *Mainliner Cleveland* having tri-colored prop tips.

Built as a DC-6B, Fleet No. 927 (N93127) was converted to a freighter after leaving the Western fleet. Its end came with TACA of El Salvador on May 2, 1975, in a crash at Altaverapaz, Guatemala.

After 17 years with United and 43,665 hours, DC-6B Fleet No. 6553 (N37553) was one of many sold to Mars Aviation which stored, then scrapped them, at Tracy, California.

Not everything on the field was four-engined equipment, of course (a favorite 1950s airline promotional phrase—over-water twins were not yet in vogue!). A different Southwest than the one which would become famous in Texas in the 1970s was using Martin 202s, while . . .

Originally a Northwest 202, N93060 came to Southwest Airways (later renamed Pacific Air Lines—see page 98) after brief interludes with Transocean and Japan Air Lines.

. . . western Regional Bonanza soldiered on with the DC-3, seen here in two different paint schemes in 1957 and 1959 *(overleaf)*, respectively.

Originally a right-hand door DC3-178 with American Airlines, by the time Bonanza received Imperial Queen *in 1955, N492 was a left-hand door DC3A. Sold to the Japanese Ministry of Transport in 1960 it was eventually scrapped after being displayed in the Tokyo area at the end of its useful career.*

Bonanza's N493 had been an original DST-318A (Douglas Sleeper Transport) with Eastern Air Lines. Like sister ship N492, it too went to Japan (with All Nippon), but ended its days more violently when it struck a mountain in the Hai Van range northwest of Da Nang on September 30, 1970, while with Air Vietnam.

Turning north along the Pacific coast finds that the classics were well represented in San Francisco as well. This time, however, the Stratocruiser belongs to the soon to be defunct Transocean Air Lines . . .

Originally operated by Pan American then BOAC, N401Q was acquired by Aero Spacelines and broken up for parts for the Guppy program.

. . . while the Pan American representative, being waved off with a flair, is DC-7C *Clipper Flora Temple.*

N739PA was later renamed Clipper Courser *with Pan American and subsequently enjoyed a career as a pure-freighter with Intercontinental Airlines, Airlift International, and the British airline Trans Meridian. It was scrapped at Miami in 1973.*

TWA 049 Constellations *(also overleaf)* **could be found at SFO, together with the carrier's early 707-131s.**

N9412H Fleet No. 520 is now resident at Nairobi Airport, Greenwood Lake, New Jersey. Intended as the centerpiece of an exotic restaurant complex which was never completed, the Connie is one of less than a handful of Model 49s left in existence.

After 16 years with TWA, N90818 Fleet No. 511 was retired with 47,542 hours in her logbook. The Model 49 is believed to have been scrapped at Las Vegas in 1964.

In contrast to TWA's Lockheed pistons, United contributed Douglas products—DC-6s, in both passenger and freighter *(overleaf)* configurations.

The 16th DC-6 off the line, N37509 Mainliner District of Columbia *racked up 15 years with United before it was disposed of to Charlotte Aircraft Corp and scrapped.*

Cargoliner San Francisco *(N37591) was the second DC-6A delivered to United in 1956. Out of use by early 1968, it was acquired by ANDES (Aerolineas Nacionales ael Ecuador SA) and is still stored at Guayaquil.*

After conceding much transcontinental nonstop traffic to rivals American and TWA, due to the 707's earlier entry into service, United lost no time in working to regain market share once its DC-8s, such as N8006U *DC-8 Jet Mainliner Captain R.L. Dobie*, arrived.

DC-8-11 N8006U, subsequently converted to a -12, then a -21, recorded 19 years with United until it was sold to Boeing as part of a trade-in for 727-200s. Like seven other sister ships, it ended its days at Kingman, Arizona.

**Martins could be seen at SFO, operated by Pacific
Air Lines in both the 202 and 404 variants.**

*Later used by Sperry Gyroscope Co for research work, Martin 202 N93060 had a shady end: impounded at Athens, Greece, for alleged
smuggling in September 1970. A few years later it had been broken up.*

Ex TWA 404 N40408 went from Pacific to Piedmont in 1966. Withdrawn from passenger service four years later, it eventually became an aerial sprayer and crashed on duty near Miami, Florida, on June 29, 1979.

Turboprops, both large and small, made appearances as well. In the former category were the F-27s of both Pacific (behind the 202s, page 98), and West Coast Airlines, two of the eventual components of Air West, Hughes Air West, Republic, and now, Northwest.

F-27 N2706 left the Hughes Airwest fleet in 1972. After some time in Saudi Arabia, it returned to the US and was used by Britt Airways.

Representing the larger category of jet props, in the form of the Lockheed Electra, are examples from Western . . .

N7137C went on to a freighter career with Evergreen International which eventually scrapped it at Marana, Arizona.

. . . and PSA. The Electra was the first aircraft bought new by Pacific Southwest. After a long hiatus, Electras would reappear in the airline's fleet during the 1970s, but not the original PSA aircraft!

After service with PSA, N171PS was converted to a freighter. It is currently with Channel Express in the UK.

By the mid-1960s, PSA had moyed up to jets, the first iteration being 727-100s, such as N975PS. Douglas DC-9s, 737s, 727-200s, L-1011s, and MD-80s would follow before the colorful carrier vanished into USAir in the late 1980s.

N975PS, PSA's sixth 727-14, was traded-in to Lockheed in 1971 on its L-1011 deal although returned to PSA for a 12-month lease the following year. After spending eight years with Hapag-Lloyd ferrying Germans to sunnier vacation destinations, it moved on to the corporate world. Currently, it is operated by the African Republic of Burkina Faso, which—as you all knew—used to be known as Upper Volta.

A pause at Seattle tends to further the impression that the Boeing 377 was a frequent visitor to the West Coast, as Northwest's N74606 *Stratocruiser Washington* gets underway.

N74606 was traded-in to Lockheed (for Electras) in 1959, after 30,497 hours with Northwest. Sold to Aero Spacelines in 1963, it was modified with a large port side cargo door in support of the Guppy program. It met the melting pot at Mojave, California.

More local to the Pacific Northwest was PNA— Pacific Northern, which billed itself as 'The Alaska Flag Line'. (One wonders how Alaska Air- lines viewed this claim.) In July 1962, you had the choice of vintage 749 Connie equipment . . .

Once Chicago & Southern's 649A City of Caracas, N86523 experienced a hard landing at Kenai, Alaska, on June 6, 1966. Considered uneconomical to repair, it was scrapped at Seattle the same year.

. . . or a modern PNA Boeing 720. Don't overlook the Alaska 880 in the background, or the Northwest DC-8 and Electra, however.

Western took over N720V when it acquired PNA in 1967 and, ironically, it eventually ended up with PNA's arch-rival Alaska Airlines. After several years of storage at Miami, it was broken up in 1984.

Capital, of course, wasn't represented at SEA, but North America's other major Viscount operator, Trans-Canada Air Lines, provided a July 1962 view of the Vickers product in the Pacific North-west. In TCA's, and later Air Canada's service, the Viscount would prove to be very long-lived, lasting until the mid-1970s.

Viscount 757 Fleet No. 648 (CF-TID) flew with TCA/Air Canada from 1959 until 1972. It then was modified by Pratt & Whitney Aircraft of Canada as an engine testbed, with a PT6A in the nose—the only five-engined Viscount! After 535 flights and 1,250 hours with PWC, it was retired in October 1989.

We won't find any Stratocruisers in Vancouver, but there was plenty of other interesting material, both conventional and exotic. In the former category for TCA are a DC-3, unusual for its use of non-integral boarding stairs, and a beautiful 1049C Constellation brought up to 'Super G' standards.

Built at Oklahoma City as a C-47A, CF-TDV Fleet No. 369 was obtained by TCA from the Royal Canadian Air Force in 1946. It ended its days in Peru, with Trans-Peruana de Aviacion SA.

Fleet No. 401 (CF-TGA) was sold to Douglas as a trade-in for DC-8s and scrapped at Burbank, California, in 1966.

The competition, Canadian Pacific, provided dramatically-lighted examples of the Convair 240 (CF-CUX) and DC-6B (CF-CZQ *Empress of Santiago*). This airline would undergo a name change in the late 1960s, to CP Air, return briefly in bilingual form (Canadian Pacific/Canadien Pacifique) to its old name, and then become one component of Canadian Airlines International.

Built for Continental as a Convair-Liner 240-3, CF-CUX Fleet No. 394, was sold to Toa Domestic Airways, Japan. Following retirement it was displayed in a Tokyo amusement park.

Built for CPA in 1956, DC-6B CF-CZQ Fleet No. 439 was subsequently converted to a freighter. Eventually it found its way to El Salvador and was operated by the Salvadorean Air Force until it crashed after take-off from San Salvador on May 1, 1986.

Both of the major Canadian carriers operated equipment which was unique to North America—the Bristol Britannia, at Canadian Pacific, and the DC-4M North Star at Trans-Canada. The latter type was powered by Rolls-Royce Merlin engines and in flight was said to be reminiscent of a formation of Spitfire fighter aircraft!

Britannia 314 CF-CZX Fleet No. 526 Empress of Montreal *saw service with CPA from 1958 until it was passed to Caledonian Airways in 1965. Subsequently used by African Safari, it was withdrawn from use in 1973 and broken up the following year.*

DC-4M2 CF-TFG Fleet No. 207 served with TCA from June 1948 until the end of 1961, racking up 38,529 hours. With several other DC-4M2s it was sold to Mexican airline Lineas Aéreas Unidas SA (LAUSA). Today, it is the last known North Star in existence, having served as the Wings Cafe at México City Airport since 1965.

Finally, what about the newest state—one which was admitted after the jet age began? In November 1963, the Inter-Island carriers (the Hawaiian equivalents of the mainland Local-Service carriers), had moved up from DC-3s, and were transporting their passengers in hand-me-down Viscounts (Aloha), and 'Super Convair' 340s (Hawaiian).

V.745D N7415 was part of the large Capital fleet of Viscounts and before reaching Hawaii, completed two years service with Austrian Airlines. Withdrawn from use in January 1971, it suffered damage in a ground fire a few months later and was scrapped at Honolulu.

Delivered to Ansett Airways in 1954, Convair 340-51A N5511K Fleet No. 30 was acquired by Hawaiian Airlines five years later and upgraded to 440 standard. It is still in service with Zantop International, as a Dart-powered 600 freighter.

A return visit to Honolulu four years later showed a further improvement in equipment, in the form of an Aloha BAC One-Eleven Series 200, prior to the airline's more lasting commitment to the Boeing 737.

After two years with Aloha, One-Eleven 215/AU N11181 Queen Kapiolani *was acquired by Mohawk. It survived a merger and a company name change, Mohawk to Allegheny, Allegheny to USAir, and was eventually retired at Las Vegas, Nevada.*

The Braniff 707-327C also is indicative of the times, as it is operating in BN's sizable MAC/PAC (Military Airlift Command/Pacific) contingent; Braniff being one of several US carriers to mount significant efforts to participate in the military airlift required by the Vietnam War.

Braniff operated N7099 from 1966 until 1972, when it was sold to Beirut-based Trans Mediterranean Airways, which still has it in its all-cargo fleet.

We hope that you've enjoyed the trip. It's evident that CO's marketing folks at LAX were not going to be outdone by their counterparts in DEN—that gold carpet is something else. It also appears that descending the Viscount's stairs in heels required poise not needed in a jetway environment.

Dubbed a Viscount II by Continental, V.812 N241V Chicago was sold to Ansett-ANA in 1960 after only two years in the US. Passed on to Far East Air Transport of Taiwan, it ended its days with Mandala of Indonesia.

in preparation . . .

VOLUME 2: INTERNATIONAL

SKYLINERS

CLIPPERS, SPEEDBIRDS AND VIKINGS

World Transport Press
Publishers of

AIRLINERS

For a fully-illustrated descriptive
catalog, write to:

WORLD TRANSPORT PRESS, INC.
P.O. Box 521238
Miami, FL 33152-1238, USA
Telephone: (305) 477-7163
Fax (24 hr): (305) 599-1995
TOLL-FREE ORDER HOTLINE
1-800-875-6711
(Continental USA only)